STUDIES IN ECONOMIC HISTORY

This new series, specially commissioned by the Economic History Society, focuses attention on the main problems of economic history. Recently, there has been a great deal of detailed research and reinterpretation, some of it controversial, but it has remained largely inaccessible to students or buried in academic journals. This series is an attempt to provide a guide to the current interpretations of the key themes of economic history in which advances have recently been made, or in which there has been significant debate.

Each book will survey recent work, indicate the full scope of the particular problem as it has been opened by research, and distinguish what conclusions can be drawn in the present state of knowledge. Both old and recent work will be reviewed critically but each book will provide a balanced survey rather than an exposition of the author's own viewpoint.

The series as a whole will give readers access to the best work done, help them to draw their own conclusions in some major fields and, by means of the critical bibliography in each book, guide them in the selection of further reading. The aim is to provide a springboard to further work and not a set of pre-packaged conclusions or short cuts.

STUDIES IN ECONOMIC HISTORY

Edited for the Economic History Society by M. W. Flinn

PUBLISHED

J. D. Marshall The Old Poor Law, 1795–1834

G. E. Mingay Enclosure and the Small Farmer in the Age of the
Industrial Revolution

IN PREPARATION

R. H. Hilton The Decline of Serfdom in England

A. S. Milward The Impact of the World Wars on the British
Economy

R. B. Outhwaite The Price Rise in Tudor and early
Stuart England

S. B. Saul The Myth of the Great Depression 1873–1896

R. S. Sayers Monetary Policy in the 1920s

A. J. Taylor Laissez-faire and State Intervention in
Nineteenth-century Britain

The Development of English Agriculture, 1815–1873

Prepared for
the Economic History Society by

E. L. JONES, M.A., D.PHIL.

Lecturer in Economic History
at the University of Reading

MACMILLAN
London · Melbourne · Toronto
1968

© The Economic History Society 1968

Published by
MACMILLAN AND CO LTD
Little Essex Street London WC2
and also at Bombay Calcutta and Madras
Macmillan South Africa (Publishers) Pty Ltd Johannesburg
The Macmillan Company of Australia Pty Ltd Melbourne
The Macmillan Company of Canada Ltd Toronto

Library of Congress catalog card no. 68–27606

Printed in Great Britain by
ROBERT MACLEHOSE AND CO LTD
The University Press, Glasgow

Other books edited by the same author
Agriculture and Economic Growth in England
1650–1815 (1967)

With G. E. Mingay
Land, Labour and Population in the Industrial Revolution
(1967)

Contents

TABLES

Preface

SO long as the study of economic history was confined to a small group at a few universities, its literature was not prolific and its few specialists had no great problem in keeping abreast of the work of their colleagues. Even in the 1930s there were only two journals devoted exclusively to this field. But the high quality of the work of the economic historians during the inter-war period and the post-war growth in the study of the social sciences sparked off an immense expansion in the study of economic history after the Second World War. There was a great expansion of research and many new journals were launched, some specialising in branches of the subject like transport, business or agricultural history. Most significantly, economic history began to be studied as an aspect of history in its own right in schools. As a consequence, the examining boards began to offer papers in economic history at all levels, while textbooks specifically designed for the school market began to be published.

For those engaged in research and writing this period of rapid expansion of economic history studies has been an exciting, if rather breathless one. For the larger numbers, however, labouring in the outfield of the schools and colleges of further education, the excitement of the explosion of research has been tempered by frustration caused by its vast quantity and, frequently, its controversial character. Nor, it must be admitted, has the ability or willingness of the academic economic historians to generalise and summarise marched in step with their enthusiasm for research.

The greatest problems of interpretation and generalisation have tended to gather round a handful of principal themes in economic history. It is, indeed, a tribute to the sound sense of economic historians that they have continued to dedicate their energies, however inconclusively, to the solution of these key problems. The results of this activity, however, much of it stored away in a wide range of academic journals, have tended to remain inaccessible to many of those currently interested in the subject. Recognising the need for guidance through the burgeoning and confusing literature that has grown around these basic topics, the Economic History Society decided to launch this series of short books. The books are intended to serve as guides to current interpretations in important fields of economic history in which important advances have recently been made, or in which there has recently been some significant debate. Each book aims to survey recent work, to indicate the full scope of the particular problem as it has been opened up by recent scholarship, and to draw such conclusions as seem warranted, given the present state of knowledge and understanding. The authors will often be at pains to point out where, in their view, because of a lack of information or inadequate research, they believe it is premature to attempt to draw firm conclusions. While authors will not hesitate to review recent and older work critically, the books are not intended to serve as vehicles for their own specialist views: the aim is to provide a balanced summary rather than an exposition of the author's own viewpoint. Each book will include a descriptive bibliography.

In this way the series aims to give all those interested in economic history at a serious level access to recent scholarship in some major fields. Above all, the aim is to help the reader to draw his own conclusions, and to guide him in the selection of further reading as a means to this end, rather than to present him with a set of pre-packaged conclusions.

University of Edinburgh M. W. FLINN
Spring, 1968 *Editor*

The State of the Art

THE rewriting of nineteenth-century agricultural history is at an awkward in-between stage. The volume and balance of the literature which has appeared in the 1960s, although still growing healthily, cannot yet sustain an entirely fresh version of developments from 1815 to 1873. The output of research has modified only in patches the conventional wisdom, as purveyed so long ago but so compellingly by Lord Ernle.[1] Other topics have quite escaped the lamps of modern enquiry. The new literature is thus not comprehensive; neither is it sufficiently focused to provide a series of ready-made debates round which a survey might be arranged. There have been a few confrontations, but no head-on clashes to rival those surrounding the early modern 'rise of the gentry' or the early industrial standard of living.

Yet reinterpretative contributions to the subject have been numerous enough and are so scattered about in monographs and journal articles as thoroughly to discomfit anyone who makes no special effort to take them into account – and to render that effort tedious for anyone out of easy reach of a university library. Here I shall try to resolve the problems of balance and limited space while discussing the new work by concentrating on four main issues. First, there is the apparent paradox that agricultural output continued to rise during the deflation of 1815–36, a phase formerly depicted as a universally crushing depression for farmers. Second, the continued prosperity of farming on arable land for a full quarter of a century after the Repeal of the Corn Laws had stripped away the tariff protection of the cereal enterprises seems to require explanation. Third, the question arises whether or not English agriculture was becoming over-capitalised during the mid-nineteenth century, depressing the rewards of land-ownership already during the so-called 'Golden Age'. Fourth, can we still accept that the condition of the farm worker remained unchangeably sombre throughout the period, with the consequence that the mushrooming of Joseph Arch's

[1] In *English Farming Past and Present*, first published 1912, 6th edition 1961.

9

union in 1872 was a final, weary act of desperation? It is round these issues, although not formulated so explicitly and certainly not decisively settled, that many of the broader reappraisals seem to group themselves. In addition, the topics themselves are broad enough to provide some overview of agricultural developments in the years between Waterloo and the super-severe arable depression which came in the 'seventies.

Configurations of Distress

AGRICULTURAL investment and activity were high during the French Revolutionary and Napoleonic wars. Bad harvests and high prices persisted year in, year out, with rising receipts outdistancing rising costs. There was a spate of enclosure by Acts of Parliament and a rapid extension of cultivation by ploughing up the hillsides and out onto the commons all over England. Farmers borrowed heavily to expand production; the country banks seemed ready enough to lend while agricultural incomes were buoyant. Rents were put up. The industry prospered.

The edge of cultivation was pushed beyond even the obliterating limits of the Second World War's reclamation campaign, so that abandoned Napoleonic ploughing rig survives far up on the chalk downs and Dartmoor and out on the New Forest heaths. Thus the potential supply of grain was much expanded, and depressed only for the time being by a fortuitous run of wet seasons. But this inflationary bubble was pricked towards the end of wartime. The harvest in 1813 was a bumper one, and with the demand for bread so inelastic the effect on prices was at once catastrophic. Wheat prices began a tumble which lasted, with brief reversals, until 1835.

Severe hurt for farmers and landowners was plain by 1815. The distress was made general thoughout rural society when 400,000 servicemen, plus an unknown number of workers from the war trades, were tossed overnight onto the shrinking labour market. Their suffering was marked by a series of riots in East Anglia in 1816.[1] The years which followed inspired some of

[1] A. J. Peacock, *Bread or Blood: A study of the agrarian riots in East Anglia in 1816* (1965).

Lord Ernle's most purple passages:

> Between 1813 and the accession of Queen Victoria falls one of the blackest periods of English farming. Prosperity no longer stimulated progress. Except in a few districts, falling prices, dwindling rents, vanishing profits did not even rouse the energy of despair. The growing demoralisation of both employers and employed, which resulted from the administration of the Poor Law, crushed the spirit of agriculturists. . . . Farms were thrown up; notices to quit poured in; numbers of tenants absconded. Large tracts of land were untenanted and often uncultivated. . . . Insolvencies, compositions, executions, seizures, arrests and imprisonments for debt multiplied. Farmhouses were full of sheriffs' officers. Many large farmers lost everything, and became applicants for pauper allowances. . . . For the next twenty years the same record of depression is continued.[1]

Ernle backed up these assertions with figures of writs and executions, making his account on the surface unassailable. Yet it was suspiciously and uniformly sombre: after twenty years of this state of affairs, would there have been any farmers left solvent, let alone any new men willing to risk apparently certain loss by entering agriculture?

The device whereby Ernle produced this alarming picture was the all-embracing generalisation. He described the experience of agriculturists all over England, whatever their system of farming, from evidence (such as figures of distraints issued for debt) taken from the worst-hit districts in the very worst spells of distress. The evidence seemed to him acceptable because he fell into the contemporary habit of debating agricultural matters almost as though wheat, the price of which was hardest hit, were the farmer's sole cash product. This partiality was encouraged by his reliance on testimonies before public enquiries – by the Board of Agriculture in 1816 and by parliamentary commissions in 1821, 1833 and 1836. To all these bodies the loudest representations were made by the big arable farmers and landowners of southern and eastern England, articulate figures of note in their own localities. These men were anxious to secure state aid, such as relief from particular rates and taxes (which tended to stick at high wartime levels while receipts from grain fell away) and security against the competition of imported cereals, something

[1] Ernle, *op. cit.*, 6th edn., pp. 319, 322–4.

11

for which many of them continued noisily to fight until their eventual defeat with the Repeal of the Corn Laws in 1846. More contented farmers, notably livestock producers from the north or west, made much less fuss. Thus it was that a primarily arable depression, and an intermittent one at that, was passed off as all-pervasive. Oddly enough, Lord Ernle himself noted that witnesses before the various enquiries were unlikely to have understated their case, but he did not allow this to tone down his stark picture of distress other than later (p. 365) to observe that it was on the clay farmers that the blow of 1813–36 had fallen most heavily.

The evidence presented to the commissions of enquiry into agrarian distress has since been more carefully sifted, county by county.[1] This produced the conclusion that the western animal-rearing districts, with counties like Lancashire and Cheshire which embraced or lay close to big urban markets for potatoes and dairy produce, barely suffered 'depression' at all. Agricultural incomes dipped unpleasantly in the rearing counties only in the worst troughs of cereal prices, when demand for their lean stock to fatten on southern and eastern arable farms sank away. Arable men simply had no spare investment funds during the spells of very low prices early in the deflation, for example in 1816 and 1821–3. Later, although the price of wheat did not stagger to its nadir until 1835, farm costs had adjusted downwards as well. This, together with a vigorous response in certain sectors of agriculture, thinned out symptoms of true distress in the later price troughs.

More recent work on the primary sources has refined our conception of the incidence of depression within the arable areas.[2] Greater descriptive exactitude has begun to uncover the kinds of internal agricultural adjustments which make possible a sketchy resolution of the paradox of the period: how to reconcile with maladjusted drops in prices and costs, which for all the revisionism were undoubtedly biting in some arable areas in

[1] G. E. Fussell and M. Compton, 'Agricultural adjustments after the Napoleonic Wars', *Economic History*, III (1939).

[2] E.g. R. A. C. Parker, 'Coke of Norfolk and the Agricultural Revolution', *Economic History Review*, 2 ser., VIII (1955), p. 158, n. 1, incidentally found that signs of strain disappeared early on Coke's famous light land estate at Holkham – a sharp fall in net income soon disappeared after 1822.

some years, the equally certain fact that production continued to climb. The per acre yield of wheat, for instance, rose by 16 per cent from 1815/19 to 1832/36.[1] The total population of England and Wales, which had been 11,004,000 in 1815, reached 14,928,000 in 1836, and this enormous increase was fed. It was fed from home supplies, with no sustained help from imports and clearly without the per capita consumption of foodstuffs falling much, if indeed it fell at all.[2] By what means did an agriculture reportedly in a state of chronic depression manage so to expand its production?

Patterns of Response

MODERN work has indicated that there were some sectors within arable farming which responded with verve to the apparently overwhelming stresses of the deflation. It is less certain what precisely the growth points were or how their manner of meeting the difficulties of the time might be combined in a single explanation. At one level, in the course of refuting the notion that the Repeal of the Corn Laws represented a straightforward victory for the urban free trade interest over the rural protectionists, Professor D. C. Moore has pointed out a dichotomy within the rural ranks.[3] On the one hand there was a section of the agricultural community which by means of improved techniques, 'were so increasing their yields and reducing their costs that they could still make a profit at prices far below those which drove their neighbours to despair'. Indeed, their expansion of output served to drive cereal prices down still farther and so intensify the price: – cost squeeze on their less

[1] M. J. R. Healy and E. L. Jones, 'Wheat Yields in England, 1815–1859', *Journal of the Royal Statistical Society*, Series A, Vol. 125 (1962), pp. 574–9.

[2] Whether the net consumption level rose or fell it seems most unlikely that either movement was very marked during the first half of the nineteenth century. Cf. E. J. Hobsbawm and R. M. Hartwell, 'The Standard of Living during the Industrial Revolution: A Discussion', *Econ. Hist. Rev.*, 2nd ser., XVI (1963), pp. 119–46.

[3] D. C. Moore, 'The Corn Laws and High Farming', *Econ. Hist. Rev.*, 2nd ser., XVIII (1965), pp. 544–61.

dynamic neighbours. The rural interest itself was therefore divided into two camps, the first of which was able by high investment in more productive techniques to meet the fall in prices by a higher output produced at lower unit costs. Here seem to have been the 'high farmers' in the sense used by James Caird, writing during the short, sharp recurrence of distress from 1849–52. The second camp comprised men who were for various reasons unable to expand their output or cut costs – Professor Moore claims because of legal impediments against the mortgaging of estates to bear the charges of agricultural improvement. This section of the farm community was held back, on this view, by the plain inadequacy of its capital inflow. It embraced the political activists who sought, in place of economic self-help, to obtain support for farm product prices or a cut in tax burdens by legislative action.

This, however, is only part of the explanation, important but incomplete because it implicitly assumes that any agriculturist who could mobilise the necessary investment capital would be able to reap the full profits of 'high farming'. The real world had a more complex structure. The physical environment of English agriculture ensured that capital, even if available, might be profitably invested here but not there. The fundamental divisions between light land and heavy clay land arable farming, and the consequences for the trends of output, have been perceived by several recent writers.[1] Only soaring grain prices and easy profits during the Napoleonic wars had reprieved the farmer on heavy clays from the long-run pressure of competition brought to bear by the technically-progressive light soil areas. This competitive struggle was renewed and exacerbated when wheat prices slumped after the wars. Contemporaries found themselves witnessing 'a fierce but silent contest carrying on between the productive lands of England

[1] David Grigg, *The Agricultural Revolution in South Lincolnshire* (1966); Alan Harris, *The Rural Landscape of the East Riding of Yorkshire, 1700–1850* (1961); F. M. L. Thompson, *English Landed Society in the Nineteenth Century* (1963), esp. pp. 216–17, 232; and J. D. Chambers and G. E. Mingay, *The Agricultural Revolution 1750–1880* (1966), p. 131. The technical disabilities of clayland agriculture have been described in detail by R. W. Sturgess, 'The Agricultural Revolution on the English Clays', *Agricultural History Review*, XIV (1966), pp. 104–21.

and the unproductive',[1] a contest which the light lands were bound to win.

The cold, stiff clays were enormously expensive to work, needing many cultivations and large horse teams. In a wet year large acreages of them went unsown. They were quite unsuitable for growing the fodder crops, especially the turnip, which had for long been colonising the lighter lands. Much of their pasture was mown to provide hay as the sole winter feed, and could not be used for profitable summer grazing. Their arable farmers battled along with the ancient clayland three-course system of two crops and a cleansing fallow, relying therefore on wheat as the cash crop, the very worst of resorts after 1815. Effective drainage, the only likely technical solution, had to await the production of cheap tile drains in the 1840s before it could begin on any scale. Here, then, was all the stuff of Ernle's account of agricultural distress.

Much of the dry-soiled uplands had come into cultivation, and their formerly empty sheep downs had been settled with new, isolated farmsteads, during the Napoleonic wars. A fringe of the thinnest such soils did go out of cultivation after the war, but the bulk responded well. Further investment there could be devoted more to improving yields than to extending cultivation, though even this did not cease in all parts. The rotations on these soils (the archetype was the Norfolk four-course) were neat successions of fodder crops and cereals, with flocks of folded sheep and in eastern England herds of yarded bullocks. The system was capable of interlinked expansion given investment at any number of points. Dung from the livestock, powerfully assisted by a big increase in the application of bone dust fertiliser (which would have washed away on the ill-drained clays) raised yields of the crops. In turn, higher yields of the forage crops fed more stock, and these gave still more dung for still more crops. Cultivation costs were low; the working season was long. Therefore it was from this sector that a rise in output, including even that of wheat,[2] came during the price fall. But lower unit costs than on the clays were probably not the only cause. In the later stages of the deflation, the prices of wool and malting barley (lightland, not heavyland, products) began to rise again. There was thus a positive incentive to produce them. It may be suggested that in

[1] Quoted by Grigg, *op. cit.*, p. 178.
[2] *Ibid.*, p. 153.

such tightly-knit rotations as obtained on the light lands, inputs designed to expand the production of these commodities would have had carry-over effects to the production of wheat. Manurial residues would help,[1] and if more sheep were kept, they could be folded on land sown to wheat just as to the other crops. In this way, the output of wheat may have risen willy-nilly.

Clearly, investment by progressive landowners and the technical advantages of lightland farming are both intimately involved in explaining the expansion of production within what Lord Ernle stamped as the black years of 1815–36. Research has not reached the point of integrating these two strands. Our information is still too spotty. Many landowners substantially helped their tenants ride out the stormy years after Waterloo by hefty but irregular remissions of rent, and by taking over the burden of farm repairs which they had tended to throw onto the tenantry during the prosperous years of war.[2] Yet we do not have sufficient data to show how far the owners of lightland and clayland estates differed in this respect. Was the truly dynamic sector of agriculture confined to the technically astute owners of unencumbered estates which happened to lie in light land districts?

Such an interpretation would perhaps narrow the base of agricultural progressives too much for them to account for the quite striking growth of output during the period. Other cross-cutting factors must have been at work. For example, although generous rent remissions evidently corresponded approximately with years of low prices, the general bursts of direct landowner investment may conceivably have occurred in the intervening

[1] E. P. Odum, studying primary production on abandoned agricultural land in South Carolina, found that it fell from 5 tons/ha. in the first year to 3 tons/ha. throughout the following six years. (*Ecology*, 41, 1960, p. 34.) There was thus a carry-over effect in year one.

[2] See e.g. Thompson, *op. cit.*, pp. 235–7. We may also note that the owners of estates were increasingly employing professional land agents, which must have raised managerial standards in agriculture. (*Ibid.*, esp. pp. 156–8, 161–2; J. Oxley Parker, *The Oxley Parker Papers: From the Letters and Diaries of an Essex Family of Land Agents in the Nineteenth Century* (Colchester, 1964), p. 136.) For another long-run force tending to support or lift the level of agricultural output – the maintenance of just adequate standards of nutrition among the rural workforce by means of the Speenhamland supplements to wages – see the final section of this book.

spells of higher prices. Investment in the latter case would not have been 'high farming' in the Cairdian sense of an attempt to combat falling prices by an increased output at lower unit costs. It would have been simple expansionism. Not enough is known about the sources of investment, its nature, or its distribution in time and place fully to account for the apparently curious growth of agricultural output at this period. Nevertheless, we can already see that the growth was basically due to some pattern of investment stemming from progressive or unencumbered sections of the landowning community, together with the competitive strength within agriculture of the light land areas. The vigour of the response, despite what we have still to learn of its origins, was outstanding – though the *caveat* must be added that output shot up even faster when prices mounted from 1837.

The Basis of the 'Golden Age'

UNTIL lately the most serious chronological gap in the coverage of nineteenth-century farming (though not of landownership) has been the third quarter. Very often, historians were inclined to pass lightly over this period as a tranquil 'Golden Age' set between the trauma of Repeal and an agonising 'Great Depression' (for arable farmers at least) which set in with the rush of cheap American wheat after the mid-seventies.[1] During this interval English cereal growers were said to have prospered exceedingly. For long their prosperity and stability, or what has passed as such, was found less enticing of study than the more drastic changes brought by the century's several runs of falling prices. The neglect is now ending and with it the original picture of undisturbed serenity for the agriculturists of the day. Nevertheless, it remains at first sight curious that so many farmers on arable land can be thought of as gaining substantially, or at least moderately, after the end of Protection. They did look

[1] Between 1870 and 1880 the proportion of wheat supplies homegrown in the United Kingdom dropped from 61 per cent to 27 per cent. (Gavin McCrone, *The Economics of Subsidising Agriculture* (1962), p. 34, table 4.)

17

back on the 'fifties and 'sixties, from the troubled final quarter of the century, as their 'Golden Age'. Why had Repeal not brought the vastly reduced wheat prices which the free traders so ardently desired and the protectionists so intensely feared?

The obvious reason why Repeal failed to bring the ruin of cereal producers in its immediate wake is that for three decades thereafter foreign competitors were in no position of undercut them. There simply was no world stockpile to cheap grain ready to pour into this country with its opening to Free Trade. The context of Repeal in the 'forties was a Europe of tight and temporarily worsening cereal supplies;[1] in the 'fifties the Crimean War interfered with Russian exports and gave English wheat growers their most agreeable years (though a passing jolt after its conclusion). English producers remained insulated from the full effects of the expansion of American resources by the lagging fall in the costs of conveying wheat from the interior United States and over the Atlantic. Simultaneously, the mid-Victorian industrial boom had inflated employment and lifted standards of living, ensuring buoyant demand conditions for many home agricultural products. Thus while the growth of supply was interrupted or retarded, demand grew more vigorously and steadily.

The vision of a farming generation for whom the bell did not toll primarily because overseas supplies of wheat were not yet abundant or could not be shipped in abundantly at competitive rates is accurate up to a point. Where it may mislead is not so much that the vision itself is too rosy as that its true origins are overlooked. A concentration on the failure of the price of wheat to sink catastrophically until the painful 'seventies produces, or depends on, the notion of agriculture as a monolithic industry in which producers shared overriding common interests, the

[1] S. Fairlie, 'The Nineteenth-Century Corn Law Reconsidered', *Econ. Hist. Rev.*, 2 ser., XVIII (1965), pp. 562–75. Note that contrary to some statements in the literature our imports of wheat from the United States *rose* appreciably during the Civil War years, when there was a temporary diversion of northern-grown grain away from the southern states, to Europe. (See M. E. Falkus, 'Russia and the International Wheat Trade, 1861–1914', *Economica*, new ser., XXXIII (1966), p. 419, n. 1.) It seems that accelerating peace-time demand for wheat within the United States may until the mid-seventies have played a bigger part in protecting the English wheat-grower than has usually been realised.

interests, that is, of grain growers. This notion is encouraged by the interminable debate about Corn Laws,[1] but it is unrealistic. Agriculture in this country comprises at least six or seven rather distinct industries which may even compete with one another. Two major groupings during the period under review were firstly livestock rearing and secondly the mixed farming of grain production plus stock fattening. To a great degree these systems were geographically separate, the rearing of store stock being located in northern and western areas, mixed farming in the south and east (except where inefficient wheat-bean-fallow rotations persisted on the heavy clays). Livestock rearing was only indirectly influenced by the level of the wheat price, yet prospered; mixed farming depended on receipts from its livestock fattening as well as from grain growing. Indeed, it was not a favourable trend of prices for wheat which underpinned the 'Golden Age' so much as the rising trend of livestock prices.

If wheat prices did not slump until the late 'seventies, neither did they show any sustained disposition to move upwards. In the short run they rose and fell sharply enough (a couple of years moderately high, a couple low) but over the thirty years these variations to all intents and purposes cancelled out. Meanwhile the general level of prices was high, and carried up with it many farm costs, a situation which pressed hardest on the expensive cereal enterprises. In particular, by the principle embodied in Engel's Law, a greater proportion of successive increments of the rising real wage of the community was spent not on the staple foodstuff, bread, where wants were first satisfied, but on the former semi-luxuries of meat and dairy produce, and perhaps on clothing since the price of wool soared dramatically. Market conditions were right for a decided swing away from wheat growing towards livestock production.[2] From the supplier's

[1] Much of this discussion has been among political historians who have greatly ignored the *agricultural* forces shaping the 'Great Debate'. The recent papers by Moore and Fairlie are important correctives.

[2] This situation and the consequent shift in the pattern of agricultural production has been independently noted by several recent writers, for example William Ashworth, *An Economic History of England: 1870–1939* (1960), and E. L. Jones, 'The Changing Basis of English Agricultural Prosperity, 1853–73', *Agric. Hist. Rev.*, X (1962), pp. 102–19. But it has also been stoutly denied, by O. R. McGregor in his Introduction, p. cxviii, to Ernle, *op. cit.*, 6th edn.

side, the new railway network made it much easier to despatch livestock to market without the serious weight losses incurred by sending them 'on the hoof', and to pick moments at which to sell.

In these circumstances, it is not surprising that the rearing districts made rapid financial strides.[1] The mixed farming areas of arable England, too, continued to fare at least satisfactorily and by most accounts very well; it appears, however, that this success did not depend on splendid receipts from wheat, but increasingly on the boost from the fatstock enterprises within the system. There was however no wholesale switch over to pure livestock production, and perhaps it was the subtlety whereby the output of animal products was expanded within mixed farming which once led writers to underplay these changes and over-emphasise the cereal side. The swing towards livestock must be taken into account, but so must the fact that it was slowed by braking mechanisms within a mixed agriculture which still placed much (perhaps too much) weight on producing wheat. An analysis of the period therefore really needs less an enquiry into how gilded the 'Golden Age' was[2] than, firstly, an appreciation of the changing structure of farming which underlay its prosperity and expansion of output, and secondly some explanation of why the bold trends of prices were not followed by quite the determined transfer into livestock production which might have been anticipated.

The strength of mixed farming during the third quarter of the nineteenth century resided in its special ability to accommodate a varying ratio of cereal to livestock product prices – so far was the period from being dominated by high, stable wheat prices. The system was an integrated one in which, if cereal prices were thought to be comparatively unremunerative, grain could be held back from the market and fed to the fatting stock in the hope

[1] See Table II, 'Price Indices for Livestock rearing farms', in E. H. Whetham, 'Livestock Prices in Britain, 1851–93', *Agric. Hist. Rev.*, XI (1963), pp. 27–35.

[2] See the comparison of agricultural income in 1851 and 1870–3 in J. R. Bellerby, 'National and Agricultural Income 1851', *Economic Journal*, LXIX (1959), pp. 95–104, though there may be some exaggeration involved in lining up the trough year, 1851, with the upswing of 1870–3.

Table 1.[1] *Relative Price Movements:* Arable and Livestock Products, 1851–80 (1865–74=100)

	1851–1855	1856–1860	1861–1865	1866–1870	1871–1875	1876–1880	Movement 1871–80; cf. 1851–60
Wheat	103	98	87	100	100	87	−7%
Barley	82	98	86	101	103	95	+10%
Oats	90	87	87	101	104	96	+7%
Beef	77	85	87	94	110	103	+31%
Mutton	80	88	93	93	108	105	+27%
Cheese	75	86	84	102	97	85	+13%
Milk	65	84	82	89	91	111	+36%

Based on E. H. Whetham, 'Livestock Prices in Britain', *Agric. Hist. Rev.*, XI (1963), p. 29, Table I; Report on Wholesale and Retail Prices, 1903, pp. 70–1, 136–7, 153. The value of wheat output per acre probably fell considerably after 1866 when below-average harvests were not fully compensated by higher prices. J. P. D. Dunbabin, 'Communications', *Past and Present*, 27 (1964), p. 109.

of better returns from this quarter. There were certainly spells in the 'fifties when wheat was cheap enough for a little of it to be fed to animals. From then on, not only did the gap between the prices of wheat and livestock concertina wider and wider apart, but very conveniently some of the passing downward bounces in the price of wheat were phases when stock prices were quite high. In this fashion, fluctuations in receipts from grain and stock tended to offset one another and (as a correspondent in the *Farmer's Magazine* remarked in 1864) the farmer's 'business position would be about an average one'. Mixed farming thus kept an approximately even keel until the end of our period, in the 'seventies, when the collapse of wheat prices showed up the system's heavy costs for labour, feed, artificials and drainage, and by bringing about a great contraction on the arable side destroyed its elegant but precarious balance.

In the interim, however, the livestock enterprises had assumed

[1] From E. J. T. Collins and E. L. Jones, 'Sectoral Advance in English Agriculture, 1850–80', *Agric. Hist. Rev.*, XV (1967), pp. 65–81.

a more important role. The mixed agriculture of the early 'seventies was quite different in aim from that of thirty or forty years earlier. Then, the livestock side had been considered supportive of the arable enterprises – that is, the fatstock had been overwintered not for their direct returns but for the dung which they supplied to the crop land. Now, despite an incomplete acceptance of the turn-about which was to prove disastrous in the 'Great Depression', receipts from their stock were already much valued by many arable men.[1]

There seems, then, little doubt that the bulk of the increase in livestock output derived from intensifying the animal enterprises within mixed farming.[2] More intensive mixed farming was made possible by the development of artificial fertilisers which were important for their root-break, and by the completion of the railway system which enabled imported feedstuffs and articials to be distributed readily throughout the country. Mixed farming extended into new districts, for instance parts of Cornwall and Cumberland, where small farmers found it ever harder to make a living solely by selling grain, but the chief mixed farming areas remained the light soils of eastern England, the Wessex chalk-lands and the Cotswolds.

Very recently, however, the case has been put forward that after 1850 the claylands underwent a metamorphosis amounting to 'revolution', and that it was from these that significant reports

[1] Because comparable annual agricultural censuses date only from 1867, we cannot trace this transition statistically. However, national figures do begin early enough to show that the swing to livestock antedates the conventional onset of the 'Great Depression' of (arable) farming in the late 'seventies. For instance, T. W. Fletcher calculates that the value of the gross output of U.K. agriculture altered as follows:

	1867–9	1870–6
Arable products	£104·17 million	£94·99 million
Livestock products	£126·76 million	£154·87 million

('The Great Depression of English Agriculture 1873–1896', *Econ. Hist. Rev.*, 2nd ser., XIII (1961), p. 432.)

[2] Except for milk, the rural production of which was stimulated by the decimation of the London dairies in the cattle plague of 1865–6. Old-established dairying districts like North Wiltshire, which had previously manufactured cheese, henceforth became alive to the possibilities of sending their milk in liquid form by rail to the metropolis.

came of an increased production of dairy produce, pigs and beef stock.[1] This advance, the argument runs, resulted from the widespread adoption of improved drainage techniques and the expanded use of oilcake and artificial manures in the 'fifties and 'sixties, improvements which permitted the hitherto backward heavy lands to surge forward during the 'Golden Age'. It is certainly true that these decades saw high investment in draining the clays – £7,381,000 of government loan funds and a large volume of private capital between 1847–72 – but much of it was carried out inefficiently, while the most experienced commentators, like Bailey Denton and James Caird, concluded that only 20 per cent or less of the land which would have benefited had been drained by 1873. And while it is undeniable that there was progress in clayland agriculture, such as some conversion of heavy Midland arable into pasture, it must be remembered that there are productive opportunities foregone for every farm enterprise replaced by another one. The evidence of expanding output of *both* cereal and animal products on the light lands is much less equivocal and it still seems that the greater part of the increase of livestock production did come from the shifting balance within established mixed farming.

This high-cost system integrating the growing of wheat with the fattening of stock, and backed by heavy outlays from landowners, thus persisted right into the 'seventies. Several writers have pointed out how vulnerable the insistence on retaining rotations in which wheat played so large a part left their operators when the ultimate crash came.[2] Despite important modifications which were stealing over agriculture, many farmers remained resistant to change. Perceiving the drift of prices, the Duke of Northumberland on his vast estates tried hard from 1863 to persuade tenants on heavy clay farms to restrict their corngrowing and lay down to permanent pasture much of their ploughland. Yet even though he offered to pay the conversion costs, they virtually ignored him.[3] Such men, and those who maintained the strict four-course rotation (an East Anglian feature which from the point of view of sheer husbandry technique was the apogee of mixed farming), were to pay dearly for their allegiance to wheat before the 'seventies were out.

[1] Sturgess, *loc. cit.*, pp. 104–5.

[2] E.g. Chambers and Mingay, *op. cit.*, pp. 185–6.

[3] Thompson, *op. cit.*, p. 255.

The rigidities which impaired a smooth, clean-cut transition to livestock farming, especially specialists' production from grass, must be spelled out if we are to grasp both the extent and limitations of change during the 'Golden Age'. They are crucial to understanding why the onrush of the 'Great Depression' was so severe for the arable community. Mixed farming was admirable at ironing out fairly minor variations in the ratio of cereal to livestock prices but quite incapable of adjusting to a massive, sudden price fall. Once again, several writers have made suggestions as to why agriculture was not fully flexible.

It is almost possible to over-explain the incomplete adjustment of agriculture to price trends which favoured greater animal production and to price prospects which made a move in that direction imperative. Firstly, there persisted in many quarters as late as the early 'eighties a curious inability to accept that crushing imports of wheat were here to stay: the masking effects of foul harvest weather at home were considered the root cause of low prices, and bad seasons could always be shrugged off as transient. Secondly, wheat growing had an almost obsessive sway over many rustic minds, yeomanly farming was expected to include it, and manure was expended on the arable to the detriment of the pasture land. Thirdly, many farmers equated technical and economic efficiency; they were conditioned to aim at the largest possible output of both cereals and livestock, which they saw could be achieved in mixed farming. Fourthly, some farmers were undoubtedly mesmerised by the self-contained beauty of that classic of mixed farming, the four-course shift, and possessed no means of cost-accounting capable of isolating the decreasing profitability of its wheat course. They had become, in a memorable but dangerous phrase, 'bucolic robots'.[1]

These psychological factors apart, there were definite husbandry constraints on expanding the livestock side. Techniques of sowing good grassland were poorly understood and not efficient in the drier areas of the south and east. Disease and weather losses (or liquidation sales of stock for which there was no feed) took an unaccustomed toll among the flocks and herds and slowed their build-up. Intensive, specialist livestock farming required smaller

[1]McGregor, in Ernle, *op. cit.*, 6th edn., pp. cxvii–cxviii. I have argued elsewhere that such men were a small (though vocal) minority. E. L. Jones, 'English Farming before and during the Nineteenth Century', *Econ. Hist. Rev.*, 2nd ser., XV (1962), pp. 148–9.

farms than did cereal growing. Bisecting an existing holding would have involved landowners in erecting a second set of buildings on one half.[1] Many of them were reluctant even to provide extra housing for livestock on the farms as they stood, something which was absolutely essential if tenants were to adapt more to animal husbandry. Unrequited tenant demand for livestock housing, especially on the clays, was one of the most general of any number of frictions between landlord and tenant during the period. Yet, despite these obstacles, there was an effort on many hands to expand livestock production, while as demand for animal products outstripped the supply the benefits of higher prices per animal were reaped by all who had beasts to sell. For all the lags, farming did not mark time: the only historical constant is change.

Mid-Victorian Investment in Land

OF the three main agricultural classes, landowners, farmers (all except 12 per cent of farm occupiers were tenants by the end of the period), and labourers, it is surprising that we know least about the economic condition of the middle group. Firsthand studies of income movements have been made as they affected landowners (partly as a tribute to their political influence) and farm workers (partly as a tribute to our political conscience), but almost none for the farming community, despite its central economic function in the countryside. Something may of course be deduced of the swings of fortune for farmers from general accounts of agricultural prosperity and distress, but only in-

[1] C. P. Kindleberger stresses the indivisibility of holdings and uncertainty about the respective shares of landlord and tenant in the transformation costs in 'The Failure of British Agriculture to Transform', *Economic Growth in France and Britain 1851–1950* (Cambridge, Mass., 1964), pp. 239–47. This deals rather more with the last quarter of the century, as does a valuable recent source book, Oxley Parker, *op. cit.*, and a valuable discussion of modern Protectionism, Michael Tracy, *Agriculture in Western Europe: Crisis and adaptation since 1880* (1964), but all three throw light on the inflexibilities which aggravated the slithering from 'Golden Age' to 'Great Depression'.

directly. What is reasonably plain is that although some sections of the farmer class managed to make satisfactory profits during downswings like that after the Napoleonic wars, others barely kept their heads above water. The commonsense view prevails that total net farm income was higher and more widely diffused when product prices were rising. This was very significant for the economy as a whole. Professor J. R. T. Hughes has stressed, for example, just how much the rise in farm incomes contributed to industrial expansion in the 'fifties, through a welling-up of purchases of machinery and other producer goods.[1] Tenant, not landowner, purchases floated the impressively bunched expansion of agricultural implement firms at this time. Iron manufacturing was a major beneficiary.

Beyond such outlines, we know little of the component (and many times contradictory) movements of income for different sets of farm producers. Here, and in the social structure, recruitment and turnover of the farm population, lies perhaps the most glaring gap in available nineteenth-century agricultural histories.[2] Plenty is known, comparatively speaking, about the sources and investment of fixed capital by landowners. But the flow of working capital to farm operators, often from sources hidden behind internal family arrangements, cannot be traced until the kinship patterns and inheritance customs of the farm community have been established.[3] The business history of the farm is unwritten.

Landowners have received the lion's share of the press. Their fortunes were clearly enormously variable in the years before Repeal and their differential ability or willingness to finance agricultural development, already touched on, was of immense moment for the agricultural economy. More landowners joined

[1] J. R. T. Hughes, *Fluctuations in Trade, Industry and Finance: a Study of British Economic Development 1850–1860* (1960), pp. 221–3.

[2] In rural history generally another virtual blank is the history of those heterogeneous groups engaged in servicing agriculture, in every capacity from blacksmiths to lawyers, and in processing farm products. David Spring has, however, published a detailed study of one strategically-placed body, the land agents. *The English Landed Estate in the Nineteenth Century: Its Administration* (Baltimore, 1963).

[3] But we have had one extremely revealing study of the role of the country banks, Audrey M. Taylor, *Gilletts, Bankers at Banbury and Oxford: a Study in Local Economic History* (1964).

26

the progressives upon Repeal, fearing that unless they equipped their farms to be run more efficiently they might lose their tenants. They were of course quite unwilling to shoulder the prodigious burden of taking their estates in hand and thus supplying all the working as well as the fixed capital, and all the managerial skills for English agriculture. Their anxiety about falling prices nevertheless proved some spur to investment, for landlords came to accept that Protection was a lost cause, like Surtees who replied to an invitation to attend a meeting of the County Agricultural Protection Society of Durham in 1851, simply 'Dear Sir – No more agitation, from yours very sincerely, R. S. Surtees' and turned to improving the farming of his own estate at Hamsterley Hall.[1] The misfortune was that strenuous investment in fixed capital proved almost as much a chimera as regards raising net rentals as Protection against the then improbable threat of a dousing by imported grain had ever done.

Professor D. C. Moore[2] has presented a case for thinking that Peel himself had in fact made a deliberate effort to stimulate cost-reducing agricultural improvements by packaging together with Repeal sharp cuts in duties on imported inputs, buckwheat, maize, clover seed and oilcake, and offers of loans for drainage. What Peel himself referred to as his 'general scheme' would therefore have been a programme to promote economic growth. Peel, himself an improving landowner[3] as well as a politician, supposedly meant to reduce the price of food while simultaneously enabling the old-established section of the landed interest to save itself. The former objective was to be attained by Repeal, the latter by galvanising the backward sector of English agriculture into effecting those cost-reducing innovations and that intensification of mixed farming which Peel's private circle of progressive landowners had already found amply profitable. Such a plan would imply faith in a kind of 'shock theory' of the diffusion of technological change, whereby the rural laggards could be forced to advance because the cold douche of Free Trade

[1] Aubrey Noakes, *R. S. Surtees* (n.d.), p. 102.

[2] Moore, *loc. cit.*, esp. pp. 553–4.

[3] In 1849 (why not earlier?) he offered his tenants an investment equal to one-fifth of the current rent in such immediate improvements as might reduce costs or increase output, together with further investment in drainage on terms to be agreed. C. S. Orwin and E. H. Whetham, *History of British Agriculture 1846–1914* (1964), p. xx.

would be at once followed by a brisk towelling in the form of reduced duties on imported inputs.

This view of the legislative context of Repeal is a well articulated and provocative contribution. There may however linger doubts as to how far Peel's 'general scheme' was a coherent programme for growth. To the present writer it still seems that Repeal was Repeal for the accepted political reasons, together with a desire on Peel's part to insure the country against famine by opening the ports to grain from new sources[1] so distant that the transport costs involved in tapping them would be high (itself suggesting that Peel had little faith in his ability to lever up home output in a short time), and that tacked on was an assortment of sops to anxious agriculturists. The ordinary farmer of the day might have been forgiven for thinking, as he did, that the compensation to home producers was less than generous. The initial sum put up for a drainage loan was a miserly £2,000,000.

Admittedly, Professor Moore contends that the loan primed the pump by advertising the opportunities for similar lending by land improvement companies. Yet of the companies founded at this time, the one set up in 1847 came to nothing, the next of 1848 ran into trouble over its legal powers and disabilities, and only the third, incorporated in 1849, really had enough powers and guarantees to be effective. It was the fourth, the Lands Improvement Company founded in the upswing year, 1853, which became the biggest lender. By 1880 it had lent over £4,000,000.[2] Peel's other positive measures were to cut tariffs on rather trivial imported items, buckwheat, maize and clover seed. Reduced duties on linseed cake and rape cake were potentially more useful, but it would have been the *existing* progressive element among agriculturists, with their intensive mixed farming systems, who would have benefited first and most from lower feed costs for livestock fed on arable farms. Peel admitted as much when he stated that clover seed was most needed 'where agriculture is most advanced'!

Further, Professor Moore implies that Peel saw himself as about to rescue the old county families from the threatening conjunction of their inertia and his Repeal – since it was the *arrivistes*, rich from capital accumulated in Victorian industry, who were best able to equip their new-bought estates to meet the

[1] Fairlie, *loc. cit.*, pp. 571–2.
[2] Spring, *op. cit.*, pp. 155–7.

challenge of lower grain prices. It would be odd if Peel saw himself as any special champion of the ancient landlords, since his own family were distinctly *nouveaux riches*, having bought their way into landed society in Staffordshire from the cotton trade. All in all, a demonstration that Repeal was simply one facet of a contrived expansionist plan probably needs fuller details of the evolution of thought within the coterie who actually drafted the Corn Importation Bill. Without that approach, almost any legislative scheme might be presented as a conscious growth endeavour by virtue of its side effects; after all, the Game Laws doubtless helped the iron industry by expanding the demand for man traps.

In any case, intentions which Peel may or may not have had to promote agricultural investment as an antidote to falling prices were overtaken by events. After 1853 the aggregate price index for farm products began to climb, and in this circumstance the strict Cairdian 'high farming' remedy for a price fall – expanding output at reduced unit costs – was irrelevant. Higher prices, increasingly skewed though they were towards animal products, brought much more general investment on the part of land-owners as well as farmers. It barely paid the landowners.

This conclusion has been persuasively canvassed by Dr. F. M. L. Thompson.[1] He points to the landowners' fixed aversion to reducing agreed rents and strong preference for financing productive improvements instead. Surtees, a landlord himself, remarked that the lowest rent a farm had been let at 'haunts it

---

[1] Most explicitly in 'English Great Estates in the 19th Century, 1790–1914', First International Conference of Economic History, Stockholm (1960), *Contributions*, pp. 385–97. The view is accepted by another specialist in the history of estate management, David Spring, 'English Landed Society in the Eighteenth and Nineteenth Centuries', *Econ. Hist. Rev.*, 2nd ser., XVII (1964), p. 149. But note that the discussion has centred on returns from rents and that landowners were also in principle the gainers by capital appreciation on their estates, even if they had no intention of realising on this. However, while farm capital rose only from £600m. to £700m. between 1865 and 1875 capital in industry, commerce and finance rose from £1,000m. to £1,600m. (See Phyllis Deane and W. A. Cole, *British Economic Growth 1688–1959* (1962), table 71, p. 274.) The great estate was thus to a large extent a social system, the opportunity costs of which were not negligible.

for evermore'.[1] The idea behind undertaking improvements was to recoup mainly by raising rents. When price prospects sparkled more brightly between the early 'fifties and the early 'seventies rents moved decisively upwards on many estates, but Dr. Thompson finds that the rise was not proportionate to the improvement outlay and sometimes even produced a yield below the rate at which the landowner had borrowed funds for the improvement. Drainage was the only innovation on which tenants customarily paid direct interest to their landlords and this was paid only when the drainage actually did bring about the permanent betterment which was aimed at. Other forms of improvement, notably new farm buildings, usually cost more in aggregate than drainage efforts but were undertaken to maintain the level of rents. The return in this shape was disappointing to say the least, an outstanding case being that of the Duke of Northumberland who laid out half-a-million pounds for a yield of about $2\frac{1}{2}$ per cent. Such paltry profits were far lower than the big landowners might have reaped in industry or commerce, from which (for reasons of social prestige) so much capital was in fact being diverted to the buying and improving of landed estates. As Dr. Thompson sums up, 'the conclusion suggested is that the biggest improvers among great landowners were subsidising agriculture, contributing directly to its over-capitalisation . . .' (1960, *loc. cit.*) and 'behind the facade of the "Golden Age of English Agriculture" which is said to have lasted for the twenty years after the outbreak of the Crimean War, a distinct weakening in the economic position of agricultural landowners can be detected'. (1963, *op. cit.*, p. 240.) Much of the heavy landowner investment of the third quarter-century was sunk for ever when the 'Great Depression' put paid to all hope of satisfactory returns, or returns at all, in the arable districts where so much of the improvement effort had been concentrated. It is said that the Duke of Bedford inspected his farms after a thorough replanning and observed gravely to a tenant named Jonathan Bodger, 'great improvements, Jonathan', to which Jonathan replied, 'great alterations, your Grace'. Although he nearly lost his farm for it, the tenant had shrewdly summed up much contemporary landowner investment.

[1] Noakes, *R. S. Surtees*, p. 162.

Returns to Labour

THE most noteworthy revised interpretations of our period probably relate to the condition of the agricultural labourer. We are still learning much of interest about the dismal level of farm worker income, parish relief, and labour mobility or immobility in the post-Napoleonic period. Two highly important critical investigations by Mark Blaug[1] have modified our views of the operation of the Old Poor Law. He urges that this was not really an instrument which demoralised the working class, over-stimulating their numerical increase and bringing about the reduction of wages. Instead, the excessive, stagnant pool of labour, especially in the arable south and east, itself pressed wages down, threatening the workers' calorific intake and hence their energy to perform their tasks. The Old Poor Law, though its out-relief was hardly generous enough to encourage breeding, fought against this tendency by building up wage levels so that, with each labourer able to put forth *some* reasonable effort, a bigger total of work got done than would have been done at the competitive wage. Market rates of pay, unsubsidised by the Speenhamland system, would have been driven too low in many over-peopled areas for farm workers to be able to buy enough food to operate efficiently. Thus by adding to earnings so that food intake was above the biologically inadequate, even if only just, the Speenhamland 'dole' increased the total labour effort, not depressed it as contemporary moralists complained.

In short, Professor Blaug's contention is that the Old Poor Law was a device with the effect of making the surplus, immobile rural labour of a still only partly-developed economy at least minimally productive. The growth of the urban-industrial sector of the English economy was not yet fast enough to absorb rural population growth, while industries in the countryside were withering away. The Old Poor Law enabled rural labour to make some

[1] Mark Blaug, 'The Myth of the Old Poor Law and the Making of the New', *Journal of Economic History*, XXIII (1963), pp. 151–84, and 'The Poor Law Report Re-examined', *Journ. Econ. Hist.*, XXIV (1964), pp. 229–45.

contribution to the economy, if only in agriculture. Prof. Blaug next argues that the Poor Law Commissioners from whose report the New Poor Law of 1834 sprang had inverted the evidence of their own 1832 enquiry to mean that the high outdoor relief of the Speenhamland system caused low wages and not vice versa. Their New Poor Law did not much change matters: twice the proportion of the population was still on relief in the Speenhamland counties in 1844 as in the non-Speenhamland counties. The brutal fact was that there was structural unemployment in the countryside, especially where seasonal unemployment was rife in the wheat-growing counties, and only the mid-Victorian industrial boom was powerful enough to disperse it.

From the 1850s the lot of the farm worker improved noticeably, though less in terms of direct spending power than in fringe benefits like allotment gardens, better cottages on the bigger estates, the provision of village schools, cottage hospitals and reading rooms.

Table 2.[1] *Regional Wage Movements, 1850–72* (Average weekly wage of all regions 1850–1 = 100)

	1850–1	1869–70	1872
Northern counties	130	165	188
Midland counties	104	138	161
Eastern counties	84	114	138
South and South-western counties	83	111	131

Based on wage data in Caird, *English Agriculture, 1850–1* (1852), p. 512; W. Hasbach, *A History of the English Agricultural Labourer* (1920), p. 284.

There were various beneficial changes such as the fading away of poaching gangs and the voluntary withdrawal of female and child labour from the heavier field work now that their menfolk could keep them. Higher wages and better social provision in rural areas were deliberately designed to hold labour on the land, for the 'Golden Age' saw an impressive movement into the expanding industrial sector precisely when farmers, expanding

[1] From Collins and Jones, 'Sectoral Advance in English Agriculture, 1850–80', *Agric. Hist. Rev.*, XV (1967).

their mixed agricultural systems, needed more hands.[1] Actual labour shortages emerged in some localities at seasons of peak demand, notably harvest time. It is utterly irrelevant that the resultant gains seem meagre and indirect by modern standards and that the farm workers' greater share of total agricultural income was still a social disgrace. What is historically significant is that the level and trend of rewards for farm labour were superior during the third quarter-century to their previous level. Not all recent authorities have brought this out. Professor McGregor writes, 'Lord Ernle characterised the years 1852–63 as "the golden age of English agriculture". The human derelicts of an industrialising society who got subsistence by working on the land would not have recognised that description . . .',[2] which, though fair in one sense, neglects the real improvement of the time. Similarly, Mrs. Orwin and Miss Whetham acknowledge briefly the mild improvement in the lot of the farm hand after the 'forties, and mention early efforts at collective bargaining in the 'sixties, but do not fully spotlight the accumulation of advances before Arch's National Agricultural Labourers' Union was formed in 1872.[3]

The conventional view has been put most forcibly by Dr. D. H. Aldcroft in a criticism of recent work by Mr. J. P. D. Dunbabin.[4] Dr. Aldcroft claims that in attempting to explain the

---

[1] E. L. Jones, 'The Agricultural Labour Market in England, 1793–1872', *Econ. Hist. Rev.*, 2nd ser., XVII (1964), pp. 322–38.

[2] McGregor, in Ernle, *op. cit.* p. cxviii. I am not here restricting the 'Golden Age' to the ten years specified by Lord Ernle, but following Dr. Thompson in applying it to the twenty years after the outbreak of the Crimean war. Other writers give various dates for the end of the 'Golden Age' or the onset of the 'Great Depression'. To my mind, the search for a sharp break between these two loosely-defined phenomena, for which the quoted names are no more than shorthand labels, is not worthwhile. Agriculture was long in shifting towards the form it adopted in the final years of the nineteenth century. There was of course an acceleration of this shift in the later 'seventies, but even then 1878 seems momentarily to have held the flood.

[3] Orwin and Whetham, *op. cit.*, chapter 8, 'The Farm Workers, 1851–1875'.

[4] In a critical note about Dunbabin's 'The "Revolt of the Field": the Agricultural Labourers'Movement in the 1870s', *Past and Present*, 26 (1963), entitled 'Communications: The "Revolt of the Field" ', *Past and Present*, 27 (1964), pp. 109–13 (including Dunbabin's reply).

timing of the meteoric 'revolt' in which Arch was the leading figure, Mr. Dunbabin neglected the deterioration of the agricultural labourers' economic position *vis-à-vis* other sectors of the community. He continues, 'mid-Victorian prosperity brought little visible gain to the agrarian worker . . . the agrarian worker was forced to take action only as a last resort'. In reply, Mr. Dunbabin is able to adduce series of wages and retail prices which demonstrate that the rise in the farm workers' real income between 1850–72 was above average.[1] The upward drift of rewards and the stirrings of unionism, pre-Arch, in the second half of the 'sixties confirm him in his belief that basically the 'Revolt' was a revolution of rising expectations. Its trigger was probably frustration at reaching a wage ceiling, or experiencing cuts in wage rates, round about 1870 when farmers in the more rigidly cereal-growing districts began to feel a price : cost squeeze on their own incomes. We are not yet sure exactly what pulled the trigger right back when the 'Revolt', in Mr. Dunbabin's phrase, 'went critical' in 1872. But it is evident enough that agricultural labour had shared in the prosperity of the 'fifties and 'sixties sufficiently to whet its appetite for more. Here, as wherever historians have been prising away the façade of mid-Victorian agriculture, unexpected symptoms of stress have come to light. The strain was acutely intensified from the later 'seventies and the resources devoted to the arable sector of English farming thereafter shrank fast away.

[1] This is supported by the calculations in J. R. Bellerby, 'National and Agricultural Income 1851', *Economic Journal*, LXIX (1959), pp. 97, 104.

Select Bibliography

The following references are intended to cover significant interpretative work published between 1960 and 1966. The former year is approximately when O. R. McGregor's valuable bibliography (in his prefatory essay to the 6th edition of Lord Ernle's *English Farming Past and Present*) was prepared. The present pamphlet was written early in 1967 and in general the literature of that year is neither considered in the text nor included here.

The place of publication is London, unless otherwise stated.

Mark Blaug, 'The Myth of the Old Poor Law and the Making of the New', *Journal of Economic History*, XXIII (1963) and 'The Poor Law Report Re-examined', *ibid.*, XXIV (1964), contends that the Speenhamland system did not depress labour effort or wages.

J. D. Chambers and G. E. Mingay, *The Agricultural Revolution 1750–1880* (1966), has become the standard text.

J. P. D. Dunbabin, 'The "Revolt of the Field": the Agricultural Labourers' Movement in the 1870s', *Past and Present*, **26** (1965), and D. H. Aldcroft (with Dunbabin's reply), 'Communications: The "Revolt of the Field" ', *ibid.*, **27** (1964), disagree as to whether the farm worker's economic condition was improving before 1872.

Lord Ernle, *English Farming Past and Present*, ed. G. E. Fussell and O. R. McGregor (London, 6th edn., 1961), was first published in 1912 and has been the chief source of the agricultural content of general histories ever since. The 6th edition carries a major introductory essay by O. R. McGregor.

S. Fairlie, 'The Nineteenth-Century Corn Law Reconsidered', *Economic History Review*, 2nd ser., XVIII (1965), surveys the European background to the 'Great Debate'.

G. E. Fussell and M. Compton, 'Agricultural adjustments after the Napoleonic Wars', *Economic History*, III (1939), reviews submissions to committees of enquiry into agrarian distress.

D. Grigg, *The Agricultural Revolution in South Lincolnshire*

(1966), is the fullest study of the divergent economic responses of major agricultural ecosystems.

M. J. R. Healy and E. L. Jones, 'Wheat Yields in England, 1815–1859', *Journal of the Royal Statistical Society*, Series A, Vol. 125 (1962), presents the results of sophisticated crop censuses carried out by Quaker corn merchants from Liverpool. The *caveat* about a (uniform) upward bias in the figures should be noted.

E. L. Jones, 'The Changing Basis of English Agricultural Prosperity, 1853–73', *Agricultural History Review*, X (1962), suggests that the 'Golden Age' was increasingly underpinned by rising returns from livestock enterprises within mixed farming.

E. L. Jones, 'The Agricultural Labour Market in England, 1793–1872', *Economic History Review*, 2nd ser., XVII (1964), suggests that all-round returns to labour were rising – however slightly – from the 1850s.

Barbara Kerr, 'The Dorset Agricultural Labourer 1750–1850', *Proc. Dorset Natural History and Archaeological Society*, 84 (1962), contains interesting suggestions about the immobility of southern labour.

J. D. Marshall, 'The Lancashire Rural Labourer in the Early Nineteenth Century', *Trans. Lancashire and Cheshire Antiquarian Society*, LXXI (1961), has important reflections on labour migration.

D. C. Moore, 'The Corn Laws and High Farming', *Economic History Review*, 2nd ser., XVIII (1965), is an engaging conception of Repeal as a programme for agrarian development.

C. S. Orwin and E. H. Whetham, *History of British Agriculture 1846–1914* (1964), is a detailed reference work.

A. J. Peacock, *Bread or Blood: A study of the agrarian riots in East Anglia in 1816* (1965), is a close investigation which suggests why Eastern England figured so little in the riots of 1830.

D. Spring, *The: English Landed Estate in the Nineteenth Century* (Baltimore, 1963), describes the administration of landed property.

R. W. Sturgess, 'The Agricultural Revolution on the English Clays', *Agricultural History Review*, XIV (1966), makes the case for a major transformation in clayland farming after 1850. This is criticised in E. J. T. Collins and E. L. Jones, 'Sectoral

36

Advance in English Agriculture, 1850–80', and defended in R. W. Sturgess, 'The Agricultural Revolution on the English Clays: a Rejoinder', *ibid.*, XV (1967).

F. M. L. Thompson, 'English Great Estates in the 19th Century', *Contributions*, First International Conference of Economic History (Stockholm, 1960), is the most concise survey of landed investment.

F. M. L. Thompson, *English Landed Society in the Nineteenth Century* (1963), is the standard source on landownership.

Index